Overshadowed by the Almighty

Understanding the Phenomenon Known as "Being Slain in the Spirit"

by

Prophetess Jackie Harewood

OVERSHADOWED BY THE ALMIGHTY

Published by:

McDougal & Associates
18896 Greenwell Springs RD
Greenwell Springs, LA 70739
www.thepublishedword.com

McDougal & Associates is dedicated to the spreading of the Gospel of Jesus Christ to as many people as possible in the shortest time possible.

ISBN 978-1-934769-99-7

Printed in the US, the UK and Australia
For Worldwide Distribution

Overshadowed by the Almighty

McDougal & Associates

Servants of Christ and Stewards of the Mysteries of God

Dedication

This book is dedicated to my daughters, Keydra De'Juan Singleton and Keyate Le'Juan Coleman, who labored with me to choose a representative image for this book. I value the great compassion you showed and the time and discussion we shared making the right decision. You are wonderful daughters who have always supported me. My prayer is that the Lord will richly bless you and your family.

Acknowledgements

I thank God for my inspiration, my friend and co-laborer in the Gospel, Apostle David Harewood, my husband. Thank you for encouraging me and supporting me in everything God has destined me to do. You have truly undergirded me, and I appreciate you and graciously respect the apostolic anointing on your life.

Frequently Asked Questions Answered in This Book

- What is the phenomenon known as falling under the power of God?
- What happens when you fall in this way?
- Why do some people fall under the power of God and others do not?
- Does God answer your request if you don't fall? In other words, is falling required to receive from God?
- What does God's voice sound like?

Whereof I am made a minister, according to the dispensation of God which is given to me for you, to fulfil the word of God; even the mystery which hath been hid from ages and from generations, but now is made manifest to his saints: to whom God would make known what is the riches of the glory of this mystery among the Gentiles; which is Christ in you, the hope of glory. Colossians 1:25-27

Contents

Introduction

Being slain in the Spirit? ...

Is it real or fake? Does something actually happen to you, or is it all an illusion? Is your body actually affected, or is it a trick of your imagination? These are all important questions that deserve answers.

I don't claim to have *all* the answers, but in the following chapters I will endeavor to answer the following:

- What is being slain in the Spirit?
- What is happening when a person is slain in the Spirit?
- What does the Bible say about being slain in the Spirit?
- Physically, why does a person fall under the Spirit?
- What does God's voice sound like?
- What should you expect when you are slain in the Spirit?
- What is a trance?
- What can you do to yield yourself to the Holy Spirit?
- Will you receive what you need from God if you do not fall under the Spirit?

Why is all of this so important to us today? 1). Because there is too much confusion on this subject in the twenty-first century Church, and 2). Because if there is a blessing to be had, those of us who love the Lord want it. Let us now begin together our journey of discovery.

Prophetess Jackie Harewood
Baton Rouge, Louisiana

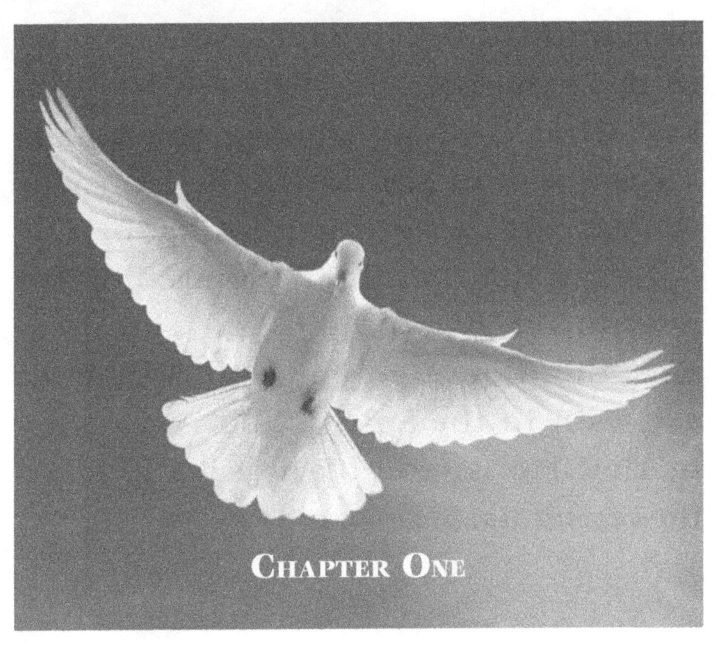

What Is Being Slain in the Spirit?

The manifestation of falling under the power of God is, first of all, an evident sign that He is among us. It is miraculous, and God does it.

While commonly called "being slain in the Spirit," some refer to this phenomenon as "falling under the power," or, as the youth of today have come to refer to it, "catching the Holy Ghost." But just what *is* being slain in the Spirit? To my way of thinking, the best way to describe this miraculous happening is to say that it is being overcome (or overpowered) by the might and presence of an omnipotent God. When we are slain in the Spirit, God is showing us that He is God by physically overpowering us.

Adam Was the First

Is this scriptural? Of course. The first time God wanted to engage man in this way, he began by putting him to sleep. Adam, the first man, was also the first to experience the power of God in this manner:

> *And the LORD God caused a deep sleep to fall upon Adam, and he slept: and he took one of his ribs, and closed up the flesh instead thereof.*
>
> Genesis 2:21

What happened to Adam that day is very similar to what happens to us when we are slain in the Spirit. God has a work He wants to do in us, and He requires that we hold still long enough for Him to do it.

God's Spirit Moves Like the Wind

This operation of the Holy Spirit, while it may be something of a mystery to us, has a sound biblical basis. Jesus explained to Nicodemus that the Spirit moves like the wind. The wind blows, He said, yet we are unable to see it. We see only the effects of the wind:

> *The wind bloweth where it listeth, and thou hearest the sound thereof, but canst not tell whence it cometh, and whither it goeth: so is every one that is born of the Spirit.*
> *Nicodemus answered and said unto him, How can these things be?*
> *Jesus answered and said unto him, Art thou a master of Israel, and knowest not these things?* John 3:8-10

The wind is not controlled or governed by our laws, and neither is the Holy Spirit. We cannot understand the moving of the wind, nor can we understand the moving of God's Spirit. As Jesus explained, although you cannot see the wind, you can see the effects of it, for you observe what it does to its surroundings.

For example, even though you cannot see the wind blowing, you can see the leaves moving in the direction the wind is blowing. By observation and deduction, therefore, you know that the wind is blowing in the direction the leaves are moving.

The Parallel Truth

Since all truth is parallel, you cannot see the Holy Spirit as He moves through your life, however, you do see the effects of His being present with you. Your character and your actions should be an indication that the Spirit is influencing your life. Before He came to dwell in you, you acted very differently. You are more godly now as a result of His presence.

Again, just as there is no law which can govern the motion of the wind, there is no law which can govern the motion of God's Holy Spirit. He does what He wants to do, whether we understand it or not.

This Book Fills a Need

For a very long time we have needed a book that explores what happens when a person is overcome by the power of God and attempts to explain the mysteries of it. Again, I do not pretend to have all the answers, but this book is a good place for a hungry heart to begin in the search for an explanation. God has promised in His Word that if we would hunger and thirst after truth, we would be filled:

> *If any of you needs wisdom to know what you should do, you should ask God, and he will give it to you. God is generous to everyone and doesn't find fault with them. When you ask for something, don't have any doubts. A person who has doubts is like a wave*

that is blown by the wind and tossed by the sea. James 1:5-6, GWT

Being Overcome Is Normal

It would be normal for God's manifest presence to overwhelm our mortal bodies in any number of ways. God is omnipresent, subsequently when you commit your life to Him, confess with your mouth, and believe in your heart that Jesus was raised from the dead for your sins, inviting Jesus to take ownership of your heart, God gives you a seal of His favor in the form of His Holy Spirit:

> *Now he which stablisheth us with you in Christ, and hath anointed us, is God; who hath also sealed us, and given the earnest of the Spirit in our hearts.* 2 Corinthians 1:21-22

The Spirit of God actually comes to take up residence in the believer. You then become spiritually minded and are under the direction and influence of the Holy Spirit:

But ye are not in the flesh, but in the Spirit, if so be that the Spirit of God dwell in you. Now if any men have not the Spirit of Christ, he is none of his.

Romans 8:9

This expression *"the Spirit of God dwell in you"* denotes intimacy of connection. We are so joined and filled with the Holy Spirit of God that typically we are not keenly aware of the power of God present within us.

Usually we do not particularly feel any different because He takes up residence in us. Despite the indwelling of the Spirit, when a door into the supernatural realm is opened for you to get a glimpse, your physical man is overwhelmed. One primary reaction is falling under the power of the Holy Spirit.

The Best Time to Connect

God wants to communicate with you, and the best time to connect with the God of the Universe is when you are at rest. When you are slain in the Spirit, you are not only at rest, but you are open and yielded, to let God speak and do what He needs to do to touch your humanity.

Needed: Yieldedness

The preferred position to get God's attention is to fall on your face, and therefore falling under the power is symbolic of surrender. In the Scriptures, God spoke to Abraham as he surrendered:

> *And Abram fell on his face: and God talked with him ... .* Genesis 17:3

Cases of the phenomenon in scripture are also referenced in Daniel:

> *His body was like beryl. His face looked like lightning. His eyes were like flaming torches. His arms and legs looked like polished bronze. When he spoke, his voice sounded like the roar of a crowd. I, Daniel, was the only one who saw the vision. The men*

with me didn't see the vision. Yet, they started to tremble violently, and they quickly hid themselves.

Daniel 10:6-7, GWT

Daniel could not continue standing because of the power and presence of God Almighty. Any of us would have responded the same given the identical situation.

Daniels' companions were also affected by the divine visitation. Although they did not see the vision, still *"they started to tremble violently."*

So what is being slain in the Spirit? It is being overcome or overpowered by the might of Him who is the Almighty.

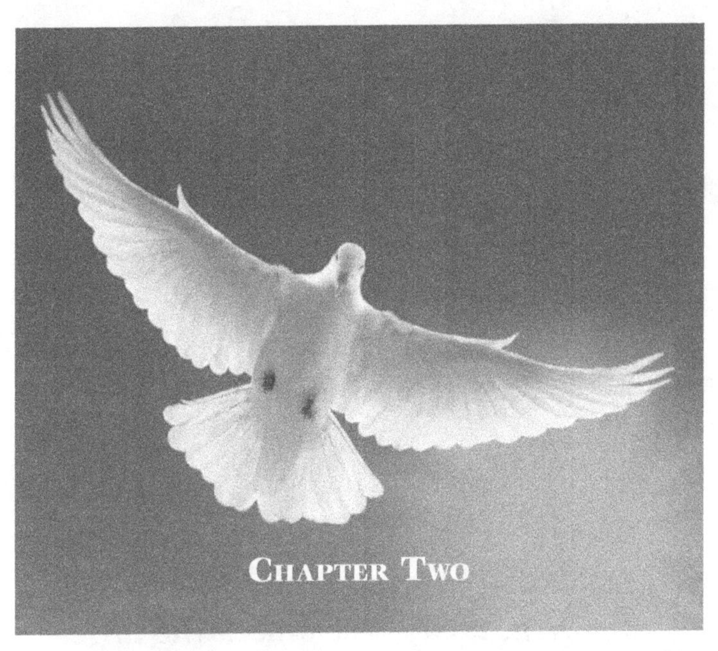

What Is Happening When a Person Is Slain in the Spirit?

What happens when a person is slain in the Spirit? For an answer to that important question, let us look at God's dealings in one particular case.

Mary Was Visited

In the beginnings of what we now know as New Testament times, God sent the angel Gabriel to Nazareth, a city in Galilee, and there the angel visited a virgin who was promised in marriage to a descendant of David, a man named Joseph. This virgin's name, of course, was Mary:

> *Six months after Elizabeth had become pregnant, God sent the angel Gabriel to Nazareth, a city in Galilee. The angel went to a virgin promised in marriage to a descendant of David named Joseph. The virgin's name was Mary.*
>
> Luke 1:26-27, GWT

When the angel arrived at Mary's home, he greeted her in a very unusual way:

> *When the angel entered her home, he greeted her and said, "You are favored by the Lord! The Lord is with you."*
>
> Luke 1:28, GWT

Mary was surprised, or, as the Scriptures describe it, *startled*, by what the angel said and tried to figure out what this greeting could mean (see verse 29). The angel then gave her a powerful and important prophetic word:

> *"Don't be afraid, Mary. You have found favor with God. You will become pregnant, give birth to a son, and name him Jesus. He will be a great man and will be called the Son of the Most High. The Lord God will give him the throne of his ancestor David. Your son will be king of Jacob's people forever, and his kingdom will never end."* Luke 1:30-33, GWT

Not surprisingly, Mary was, again, startled by what she heard. She had been startled at the appearance of the angel, and now she was startled by what he was saying. His words didn't seem to make sense to her, specifically because she was a young unmarried woman:

Mary asked the angel, "How can this be? I've never had sexual intercourse."

Luke 1:34, GWT

God always chooses to use the ordinary, modest, and least likely to succeed person, and so Mary was in position and available for His use. It is promising to note that God will use anyone with a pure heart. He is still looking for people with a virgin spirit.

In the natural, being a virgin refers to a person who has never had sexual intercourse. It can also refer to someone who has taken a vow of chastity for religious reasons.

What Is Chastity?

Let me clarify this word *chastity*. According to *Merriam-Webster's Dictionary*, chastity is "abstention from all sexual intercourse and personal integrity." We who have been washed in the blood of Jesus can identify with being a virgin, for His blood washes away our sins and makes us as if we had never sinned. In Christ, our sins are not only forgiven; they are also forgotten, as if they had never existed in the first place.

Then, because of our love for Christ, as we vow to abstain from worldly lusts, we present ourselves to the Father as a living sacrifice. God then sees us as being spiritual virgins and impregnates our hearts with His vision:

> *Brothers and sisters, in view of all we have just shared about God's compassion, I encourage you to offer your bodies as living sacrifices, dedicated to God and pleasing to him. This kind of worship is appropriate for you. Don't become like the people of this world. Instead, change the way you think. Then you will always be able to determine what God really wants — what is good, pleasing, and perfect.* Romans 12:1-2, GWT

When we desire the perfect will of God and make ourselves available to Him with a pure heart, He can then impregnate our hearts. In this process, we, of course, are not impregnated with a physical embryo but, rather, with a spiritual vision, which leads to a fruitful destiny.

This is such a wonderful subject that I could continue in this vein, but since the book is dedicated specifically to exploring the phenomenon of falling under the power, let's leave it at that for now.

What Are We Getting At?

So, what are we getting at in relation to our subject by looking at the story of Mary? Let's go a little further:

> *And the angel answered and said unto her, The Holy Ghost shall come upon thee, and the power of the Highest shall overshadow thee: therefore also that holy thing which shall be born of thee shall be called the Son of God.*
>
> Luke 1:35

When God is ready to impregnate you with a vision, He will overshadow you.

When He wants to move you on to the next step closer to your purpose, He will overshadow you. In this way, He advances you toward your destiny by giving you fresh revelation of your next sequential action.

In Mary's case, she became pregnant with the Holy Child Jesus. In your case, in this New Testament era, you conceive a holy thing in the form of a vision.

Receiving the Desires of Your Heart

God has said in His Word that He would give us the desires of our heart:

> *Delight thyself also in the* LORD*; and he shall give thee the desires of thine heart.* Psalm 37:4

The word *delight* here is from the Hebrew word *amag*, which is derived from a primitive root which means "to be soft or pliable." God is looking for committed people who are flexible and willing to change their current direction.

He is looking for individuals who are open to taking risks and bold enough to exercise authority for the sake of the Kingdom.

The moment you stop concentrating on your self-imposed assignment (any assignment you may have given yourself) and receive the assignment that God gives, the results will be positive. God gives assignments designed to move you into your destiny.

All your energy should be expended toward working the vision God has given you. When busy, insignificant things clutter your life, you lose sight of the real plan for your life. Any effort that does not move you toward your goal will move you further away from that goal.

When God can trust you, He will give you the desires of your heart. Giving you those desires is not difficult for Him because He put them there in the first place.

What Does It All Mean?

Does all of this have something to do with being slain in the Spirit? Yes, it does. I believe that when a person falls under the power of God, He sends the Holy Ghost to overshadow that person and instill in them the vision He desires. This vision might be a ministry venture, a bold, new business venture, or any number of other things. These new thoughts from God are His seeds that now impregnate your heart.

Your Fertile Time

In the natural sense, when a woman wants to get pregnant, there are signs that indicate her fertile time of the month. And, since all truth is parallel, in the Spirit, a sign indicating that you are spiritually fertile is a feeling of unsatisfied-satisfaction deep within your heart. This lets you know that your spirit is ready to be impregnated by the Holy Spirit.

When you have fallen under the power of God, the womb of your spirit is opened and made ready for the Holy Ghost to overshadow you. Then He can come and impregnate you with your divine destiny.

What Does Overshadowed Mean?

What does it mean to be overshadowed? A shadow is created when an object stands in rays of light. The Holy Ghost stands in the presence of Father God on our behalf, and His job is to take from Father God and give to us:

> *Howbeit when he, the Spirit of truth, is come, he will guide you into all truth: for he shall not speak of himself; but whatsoever he shall hear, that shall he speak: and he will show you things to come. He shall glorify me: for he shall receive of mine, and shall shew it unto you. All things that the Father hath are mine: therefore said I, that he shall take of mine, and shall shew it unto you.* John 16:13-15

In the natural, the size of the shadow, whether large or small, is determined by the object moving closer to the light source or further away from it. Since all truth is parallel, in a spiritual sense, the work of the Holy Ghost will be in proportion to the degree you draw closer to God and let His light shine more directly on you.

When you are slain in the Spirit, the Holy Ghost stands in the glorious light of the Father, casting a shadow upon you. Thus, the power of the Highest overshadows you, resulting in the impregnation work of the Lord being done in your spirit.

You Are Covered

When you are overshadowed, it is a type of being hidden in God's power. You are covered under the shadow of His presence:

> *His brightness is like the sunlight.*
> *Rays of light stream from his hand.*
> *That is where his power is hidden.*
>
> Habakkuk 3:4, GWT

The brilliance of God's light is the glory of His presence.

How It Happens

Being overshadowed can happen in several different ways. From my experience, being overshadowed can be felt when you sense His presence in your everyday activities. You may be engaged in regular, daily chores, yet you feel as if there were a cloak over you.

The word *power* suggests that the Holy Ghost comes upon you, overshadows you, and miraculous power is generated from Him. That miraculous power has the ability to create miracles in your life. If you need a miracle in your body or spirit, He may generate the miraculous power to grant the physical or emotional healing you need. When you experience that miraculous power, you have received a divine intervention from God.

A divine intervention is the process God uses to prepare your spiritual womb to conceive the seed. In this case, the seed is a holy thing. As noted earlier, this seed could be a vision, an assignment, a profession, a ministry, or it could even be a long-awaited companion. The miraculous comes into clearer focus once you have received the seed, and the seed itself comes with the revelation and inspiration needed to bring that holy thing to reality.

Coming To Full Term

After God releases that holy thing in your spiritual womb, it must come to term. In natural childbearing, full term is nine months. In a spiritual sense, full term could be as short as nine days, it could take a few months, or it could take years. Only God can determine the right length of time for a vision to come to fruition. Whatever the case, God will not let you abort, nor will He bring your seed to birth until it is fully developed and has the capacity to sustain life and thrive.

Life can be sustained without evidence of thriving. To *thrive*, according to *Merriam-Webster,* means "to grow vigorously, to gain in wealth or possessions; to progress toward or realize a goal despite or because of circumstances." God will not only bring that holy thing to life, but you should prosper, or flourish, in your destiny.

A Holy Heaviness

At other times you may feel heaviness in your spirit, at the same time you sense that it is not something negative. You cannot identify any reason you may be experiencing that feeling. This could very well be the glory of God resting upon you:

> *And there I will meet with the children of Israel, and the tabernacle shall be sanctified by my glory.*
>
> Exodus 29:43

In Old Testament times, the tabernacle was sanctified by God's glory. In our New Testament era, *you* are the tabernacle of the Holy Spirit of God. Therefore it is safe to believe that the glory of the Lord can sanctify *you*, setting you apart for the Lord and His work.

When you are slain under the power of the Holy Ghost, He has a chance to impart wisdom and knowledge to your spirit. As you lie quietly before Him, He will have time to speak to you and work in you.

Receiving from the Spirit of Truth

The Holy Spirit is also known as the Spirit of Truth. When you are slain in the Spirit, the Spirit of Truth is communicating with the Father on your behalf. His responsibility is to guide you into all truth.

This word *guide* (in the Greek) is *hodēgeō* from *hodegos*, which means "to show the way." Therefore, while you are slain in the Spirit, God's Spirit can show you the right path to take. He can show you the next step toward your destiny.

It is important that we not be too quick to get up when we fall under the power of God because the Holy Spirit may want to show us something. At the opportune time, you will emerge with full knowledge and great revelation with the necessary information to take the next step toward your future reign of victory and success. Give God whatever time He requires.

Communicating Spirit to Spirit

God is a spirit, and we are spirit, yet we live in a body. You can only communicate with God through your spirit. When God wants to communicate with you, He must speak directly to your spirit, and the Holy Spirit translates from spirit to natural (your intellect) what God is saying to you.

An illustration might bring this important truth into clearer focus. When you try to communicate with an individual who does not speak your language, a natural language barrier exists. The only way the two of you can communicate would be: 1). For you to learn the language of that person or for them to learn your language, or 2). To make use of an interpreter. Since learning a language takes time, usually using an interpreter is the logical solution for communicating with an individual who does not speak your language.

Since all truth is parallel, and God speaks directly to your spirit, you could say that He speaks spirit language. If you are baptized in the Holy Ghost, you speak in the spirit (in other tongues). The challenge here is that you cannot know what your spirit is saying because it is speaking a spirit language. You will not be able to know what your spirit is saying without the assistance of someone who speaks that particular language.

That Someone Is the Holy Spirit

That Someone is the Holy Spirit; because He is a spirit, He speaks spirit language. The advantage is that He is multilingual. He speaks both spirit language and the human languages. The Holy Spirit then interprets in the language a person understands. If you speak German, He interprets in German, if in English, then He interprets in English, if in Spanish, then in Spanish, etc. The Holy Spirit's job is to hear in the spirit and interpret what God is saying in a language which you can relate to:

Even so ye, forasmuch as ye are zealous of spiritual gifts, seek that ye may excel to the edifying of the church. Wherefore let him that speaketh in an unknown tongue pray that he may interpret. For if I pray in an unknown tongue, my spirit prayeth, but my understanding is unfruitful.

1 Corinthians 14:12-14

Notice that the Scriptures use the term *unknown tongue.* This term denotes a language that has not been acquired naturally. The Holy Spirit translates for the believer because He is knowledgeable in every language. The Holy Spirit, as the third person of the Godhead, is omniscient, meaning that He knows all things.

Your Opponent

There is an opponent contending against you who is set to destroy the implanted seed deposited into your spiritual womb by the Holy Spirit. That opponent, of course, is Satan.

The seed must be strong enough at birth to carry out the vision God has assigned to it. Satan's mission is to contradict the seed that has been conceived. Your seed must mature, be nurtured, and kept until it is strong enough to stand on its own.

For some, your vision is at an infant stage; for others your seed has been tested, tried, and is now ready to be discovered. Wherever you may be in the process, remain faithful, and God will see you through, for His glory and for your good.

Remain Alert to Protect the Seed

We all have this common enemy, Satan, the accuser of the brethren. This fact is common knowledge. Therefore every believer must remain alert to protect their seed at all costs:

> *And I heard a loud voice saying in heaven, Now is come salvation, and strength, and the kingdom of our God, and the power of his Christ: for the*

accuser of our brethren is cast down, which accused them before our God day and night. Revelation 12:10

What is not commonly known is that if the adversary cannot cause you to abort the seed God has planted in you, he will often distort that seed (that vision). He has many ways of doing this. One of the ways he uses to distort your vision is to cause you to rely on wrong counsel and premature advice. Misdirected guidance and perverted direction are also techniques he uses.

Satan's Most Damaging Tactic

Satan's most damaging tactic is to lull you into sitting in a particular church just to please someone else. Friends and family members can cause you to be stunted in your growth in the Kingdom. At other times, pride will keep you from advancing. You may prefer to remain at a place where certain people fellowship in order to advance your career. This may well advance your profession, but it can also be spiritually disastrous.

An even more detrimental tactic Satan uses is to hypnotize you into sitting in a church that does not recognize your gifts, talents, and abilities. I have known individuals who were intent on staying in a given church despite the fact that they were not being given any help in developing their gift. They knew God had called them to operate in certain gifts, but they agreed to remain in a place where those gifts could not be exercised.

People like this end up having to spend much time visiting other houses of worship, just to get fed, and yet they return to their prison house of worship, fooling themselves into thinking that they are somehow contributing in that place.

Tragically, these are good Christians, and they think it important not to leave their secure place, only to find years later that they are still on the same spiritual level. Their church has done nothing to steer them in the direction of their calling.

My advice to these people is: Act Now! Rebuke the spirit of fear. Then get up and find the place of development God is leading you to. The longer you stay in a dormant state, the longer it will take for you to get started developing your vision:

> *And we know that all things work together for good to them that love God, to them who are the called according to his purpose.* Romans 8:28

Satan Will Try To Confuse the Timing

In an attempt to distort your vision, Satan will introduce you to opportunities that cause you to either move ahead of God's time or behind it. If all else fails, He may lead you in the wrong direction or get you to settle for less than what God has spoken to your spirit.

Another Sabotage Technique

Another common sabotage technique is diversion. The enemy causes a diversion by sending people to consume your time. These people are being influenced by a familiar spirit and do not have a clue that they are being used by Satan to distract you from your goal.

Beware when you have gotten serious about pressing into the things of God, and an old friend or acquaintance shows up to consume your time and distract you. Don't be fooled into thinking that this person with so many problems really wants or intends to accept your advice. They are just time wasters, sent by Satan as a diversionary tactic.

If anyone takes up an excessive amount of your time, know that they are a decoy from Satan. If you work with that person for a reasonable amount of time and still don't seem to be making any headway, then you are not the one to help them. God has someone else who can be more effective.

The more time you spend with such people, the more you will delay their breakthrough. And, more importantly, the time you spend with them takes up the time God has designed for you to come into the fullness of your own spiritual life.

If any person can prevent you from being available to walk into your calling, then Satan will send them your way. A familiar spirits' strategy is to entice you. Its job is to maximize your time with anything other than what will lead to the fulfillment of your destiny.

Get Into a Church Where You are Supported

As noted earlier, another way the adversary tries to distort the vision is to cause you to rely on wrong counsel, premature advice, misdirected guidance and perverted direction. You need to be in a church where you are supported and encouraged to pursue purpose and to advance in your calling. Guard against inattention and neglect of God's assignment. Being in the right place of worship will bring you into alignment with your calling and will determine the height, depth, and width of a successful outcome.

Your goal should be to find a church that contributes to your growth in the Kingdom of God. Church is a place for individuals with "*like precious faith*" and it is a proving-ground to elevate you.

Therefore we ought to give the more earnest heed to the things which we have heard, lest at any time we should let them slip. Hebrews 2:1

Peter Wagner, in his book, *Your Spiritual Gifts Can Help Your Church Grow*, states that he does not recommend that people decide to stay where they are and try to convince the church or certain people in it to change *their* position. The energy such activity saps from the church is enormous. Move on, he says.

"God did not give spiritual gifts for dissension and hard feelings. He gave them to enhance the health, vitality, and growth of the entire Body. Every unit of spiritual energy being used to fight battles over spiritual gifts is one unit that cannot be used for ministry to the lost."[1]

So what is happening when a person is being slain in the Spirit? God is overshadowing them and implanting a holy seed within their spirit.

1 Wagner, Peter, *Your Spiritual Gifts Can Help Your Church Grow* (Ventura, California, Regal Books: 2012).

What Does the Bible Say about Being Slain in the Spirit?

What does the Bible say about being slain in the Spirit? Interestingly enough, the term "being slain in the Spirit" is not to be found in the Bible. It is a term commonly used within modern Charismatic

Christianity that describes "a religious behavior in which an individual falls to the floor."[2] This usually happens during a personal encounter with the Holy Spirit, and is often associated with the laying on of hands.

When a person experiences this phenomenon of being slain in the Spirit, they may receive a vision, receive revelation, receive instruction from God, or receive healing. Many people testify that God spoke to them in some fashion while they were on the floor.

Common in Early America

But being slain in the Spirit did not begin in this modern era. It was extremely common in early America in the late eighteenth century, being a common occurrence at campmeetings and love feasts. At the time, it was referred to as, "falling under the Spirit's power," "falling before the Lord," or "resting in the Spirit."

2 http://dictionary.reference.com

And the phenomenon of being slain in the Spirit goes back much further in church history. Under John Wesley's preaching in the 1700s people "... were struck to the ground and lay there groaning," an occurrence which also accompanied the preaching of Methodist circuit-rider, Peter Cartwright, not to mention George Whitefield, Jonathan Edwards, and Charles G. Finney.[3]

As Thomas Csordas, Professor of Anthropology at the University of California San Diego, has said: "In Charismatic ritual life, resting in the Spirit can serve the purposes of demonstrating divine power; or exhibiting the faith of those who are 'open' to such power; or allowing a person to be close to, touched by, or spoken to, by God ... or preparing a person to receive and exercise a spiritual gift; or of healing."[4]

In Bible Days

Even though the Bible does not use the exact words we use today to describe this

3 Ibid
4 http://www.merriam-webster.com

phenomenon, falling in the Spirit was experienced by those in Bible days. Falling while in the presence of God was, at times, also accompanied by manifestations of trembling, physical weakness, and deep sleep known as a trance (more will be said of trances in Chapter Eight).

Biblical Examples

References to falling as the result of feeling overwhelmed by the divine presence of God are found in Numbers 22:31, Judges 13:20, Ezekiel 1:28, 3:23-24, 43:3, and 44:4-5, Daniel 8:17-19, and Matthew 17:5-6, among other places:

> *Then the* LORD *opened the eyes of Balaam, and he saw the angel of the* LORD *standing in the way, and his sword drawn in his hand: and he bowed down his head, and fell flat on his face.* Numbers 22:31

> *For it came to pass, when the flame went up toward heaven from off the*

altar, that the angel of the LORD ascended in the flame of the altar. And Manoah and his wife looked on it, and fell on their faces to the ground. But the angel of the LORD did no more appear to Manoah and to his wife. Then Manoah knew that he was an angel of the LORD. Judges 13:20-21

As the appearance of the bow that is in the cloud in the day of rain, so was the appearance of the brightness round about. This was the appearance of the likeness of the glory of the LORD. And when I saw it, I fell upon my face, and I heard a voice of one that spake. Ezekiel 1:28

Then I arose, and went forth into the plain: and, behold, the glory of the LORD stood there, as the glory which I saw by the river of Chebar: and I fell on my face. Then the spirit entered into me, and set me upon my feet, and spake with me, and said unto me, Go, shut thyself within thine house.

Ezekiel 3:23-24

> *And it was according to the appearance of the vision which I saw, even according to the vision that I saw when I came to destroy the city: and the visions were like the vision that I saw by the river Chebar; and I fell upon my face.* Ezekiel 43:3

In all of these instances, the Scriptures repeatedly mention the effect of experiencing the supernatural.

Falling on Your Face

So experiencing the power of God can move you to fall on your face:

> *Then brought he me the way of the north gate before the house: and I looked, and, behold, the glory of the LORD filled the house of the LORD: and I fell upon my face. And the LORD said unto me, Son of man, mark well, and behold with thine eyes, and hear with thine ears all that I say unto thee concerning all the ordinances of the*

house of the LORD, *and all the laws thereof; and mark well the entering in of the house, with every going forth of the sanctuary.* Ezekiel 44:4-5

So he came near where I stood: and when he came, I was afraid, and fell upon my face: but he said unto me, Understand, O son of man: for at the time of the end shall be the vision. Now as he was speaking with me, I was in a deep sleep on my face toward the ground: but he touched me, and set me upright. And he said, Behold, I will make thee know what shall be in the last end of the indignation: for at the time appointed the end shall be.

Daniel 8:17-19

While he yet spake, behold, a bright cloud overshadowed them: and behold a voice out of the cloud, which said, this is my beloved Son, in whom I am well pleased; hear ye him. And when the disciples heard it, they fell on their face, and were sore afraid. Matthew 17:5-6

So, what does the Bible say about being slain in the Spirit? Plenty. Clearly, this is not a new phenomenon. It has happened in every generation and is a very biblical phenomenon.

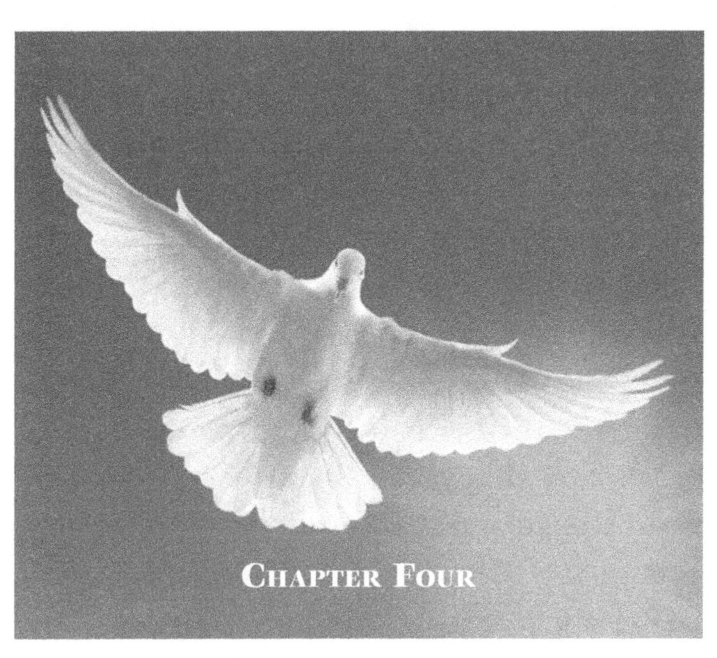

Physically, Why Does a Person Fall Under the Power?

Physically speaking, why does a person fall under the power of God? Can this phenomenon be explained? What would cause someone to simply fall down in God's presence?

The presence of God can unquestionably produce electrifying results. A slight touch from the omnipotent God causes your emotions to be overcome, and the body's way of coping with this overwhelming experience is to collapse. The power of God, thus, produces the dramatic effect of falling down as if becoming unconscious.

When the Holy Spirit comes upon you, the result is a touch of God's glory. His glory fills you until there is a sense of being positively overwhelmed. You feel the peace of God, and healing and restoration is extended to you each time you yield to the Holy Spirit in this way.

Still, when you fall under the power of God, you usually remain conscious and awake. You may even hear sounds around you. You may also hear the voice of God as you experience His love. Your spiritual senses are heightened, and this gives you the benefit of being connected to your spiritual senses.

The Five Senses

The physical body has five senses that interact with the environment: taste, touch, smell, sight, and sound. According to 1 Thessalonians 5:23, we are triune beings, made up of body, soul, and spirit:

> *And the very God of peace sanctify you wholly; and I pray God your whole spirit and soul and body be preserved blameless unto the coming of our Lord Jesus Christ.* 1 Thessalonians 5:23

Your physical senses, therefore, interact with your soul. The soul realm is made up of your mind, will, emotions, and memory. Therefore a smell brings back a memory. The spirit also has five senses that interact with your spirit.

The soul and spirit senses are just as important as the physical senses. Unfortunately most individuals have not developed these senses. The Bible makes it clear that you have these senses. Let's look at them more closely.

Spiritual Taste

Using Ezekiel 3:1-3 as a reference suggests that if you taste something sweet, sour, or salty, yet have not had anything to eat, you should ask the Lord if He is trying to speak to you. On occasion, God spoke through experiences with spiritual taste:

> *Moreover he said unto me, Son of man, eat that thou findest; eat this roll, and go speak unto the house of Israel. So I opened my mouth, and he caused me to eat that roll. And he said unto me, Son of man, cause thy belly to eat, and fill thy bowels with this roll that I give thee. Then did I eat it; and it was in my mouth as honey for sweetness.*
>
> Ezekiel 3:1-3

Several scriptures either regard or imply the use of spiritual senses:

> *Is there iniquity in my tongue? cannot my taste discern perverse things?*
>
> Job 6:30

O taste and see that the LORD is good: blessed is the man that trusteth in him. Psalm 34:8

This familiar scripture implies that God's Word provides an experience that satisfies our longings. It is *"sweeter than honey"*:

How sweet are thy words unto my taste! yea, sweeter than honey to my mouth! Psalm 119:103

For centuries, honey has been used to treat all sorts of ailments. It can be applied topically to heal wounds and rashes, or it can be taken internally to treat infections and address other health concerns.[5] Many people drink a mixture of vinegar and honey every day and swear by its benefits.

All truth is parallel: the Word of God is beneficial for every ailment. Just as honey treats multiple aliments, so God's Word is even more effective in its application. For instance, we are told:

---

5 http://www.naturalnews.com/035493_raw_honey_health_benefits_antibacterial.html#ixzz2Q4HZiy5W

That he might sanctify and cleanse it with the washing of water by the word.
Ephesians 5:26

Spiritual Smell

I often smell a sweet fragrance when the presence of the Lord comes into a room, as if someone has sprayed air freshener. This is not unusual. Many have this same experience. God's Word declares:

But I thank God, who always leads us in victory because of Christ. Wherever we go, God uses us to make clear what it means to know Christ. It's like a fragrance that fills the air.
2 Corinthians 2:14, GWT

When you give to the work of the Lord, to advance the Kingdom, that gift is said to have a sweet odor that is released into the atmosphere:

But I have all, and abound: I am full, having received of Epaphroditus the things which were sent from you, an odour of a sweet smell, a sacrifice acceptable, wellpleasing to God.

Philippians 4:18-19

As this scripture states, the Lord also smelled the sweet savor and was pleased. He responded in this way to the sacrifice offered in faith by righteous men such as Noah, and found it as acceptable as a most fragrant incense.[6] To God, the physical act of sacrifice is experienced as a smell. Each time you offer to Him what is important to you, He sees it as a sweet fragrance:

And the LORD smelled a sweet savour; and the LORD said in his heart, I will not again curse the ground any more for man's sake; for the imagination of man's heart is evil from his youth; neither will I again smite any more everything living, as I have done.

Genesis 8:21

---

6 David Brown, Robert Jamison and Andrew Robert Fausset, *A Commentary: Critical, Experimental, and Practical on the Old and New Testaments* (Philadelphia : J. B. Lippincott, 1866).

Spiritual Touch

There was an occasion when Jesus was almost physically crushed, but He didn't react. When someone touched His spirit, He responded immediately. He hadn't commented at all on the activity of the crowd of people who had nearly crushed Him, but He commented on the touch He felt in His spirit from a single woman.

When this woman touched His physical garment, she released her faith. The release of her faith penetrated the physical realm of His garment and activated His virtue. Jesus felt and responded to this touch in His spirit:

> *And a woman having an issue of blood twelve years, which had spent all her living upon physicians, neither could be healed of any, came behind him, and touched the border of his garment: and immediately her issue of blood stanched. And Jesus said who touched me?*
>
> *When all denied, Peter and they that were with him said, Master, the*

multitude throng thee and press thee, and sayest thou, who touched me? And Jesus said, Somebody hath touched me: for I perceive that virtue is gone out of me. Luke 8:43-46

Spiritual Sight

At one point in the life of the prophet Elisha, the Syrians were sent to seize him, and he and his servant were surrounded by them. With his physical eyes, the servant saw the danger and reacted. To combat this danger, Elisha prayed that the Lord would open his servant's spiritual eyes:

And Elisha prayed, and said, LORD, I pray thee, open his eyes, that he may see. And the LORD opened the eyes of the young man; and he saw: and, behold, the mountain was full of horses and chariots of fire round about Elisha. 2 Kings 6:17

Seeing with your spiritual eyes is like scaling a wall by faith and then being able to peer over into a whole new dimension.

The spirit realm cannot be seen by the natural eye, and, as the Scriptures declare, without faith it is impossible to please God, for without it, it is impossible for you to see with spiritual eyes, eyes of faith:

> *But without faith it is impossible to please him: for he that cometh to God must believe that he is, and that he is a rewarder of them that diligently seek him.* Hebrews 11:6

The stronger your faith, the clearer your spiritual sight will be. The more you trust your spiritual sight, the less you will need to depend on what you see in the natural real.

When you realize that the whole universe, under God's direction, is working for you in the unseen realm, the more confidence you will have for a victorious outcome. It is your belief in God's Word and your assurance in Him making that Word come alive in your life that elevates you.

The truth is: the unseen realm works with unseen forces that fuel your dilemma.

Never forget that your anointing and the spirit world are always at work on your behalf. Make a decision today to put a demand on 2 Kings 6:17. Pray that your eyes would be open to the spirit realm:

What Happens

All of this interaction in response to the moving of the Holy Spirit in your life leads to being slain in the Spirit. In the Old Testament, we have the following account:

> *And it came to pass, when the priests were come out of the holy place, that the cloud filled the house of the LORD, so that the priests could not stand to minister because of the cloud: for the glory of the LORD had filled the house of the LORD.* 1 Kings 8:10-11

This cloud was symbolic of the presence of the Lord. The intensity of it struck the spirit and the mind of the priests, and they were overcome to the point of collapsing under the power of God.

The same thing happened in New Testament times. For instance, the keepers of the tomb of Jesus *"became as dead men"* when a mighty angel came to visit:

> *In the end of the sabbath, as it began to dawn toward the first day of the week, came Mary Magdalene and the other Mary to see the sepulchre. And, behold, there was a great earthquake: for the angel of the Lord descended from heaven, and came and rolled back the stone from the door, and sat upon it. His countenance was like lightning, and his raiment white as snow: and for fear of him the keepers did shake, and became as dead men.*
>
> Matthew 28:1-4

One of the reactions that take place when a person comes into contact with the divine realm is that their body begins to shake. Then it collapses.

John recorded the fact that when Jesus acknowledged Himself as *"I am"* during His arrest, those who had come to take

Him captive were suddenly slain in the Spirit:

> *As soon then as he had said unto them, I am he, they went backward, and fell to the ground.* John 18:6

Spiritual Intoxication?

There are times when you may feel intoxicated or you may experience light-headedness in the presence of God. The very disciples of Jesus appeared drunk after the outpouring of the Spirit at Pentecost, and Peter had to explain it to bystanders:

> *For these are not drunken, as ye suppose, seeing it is but the third hour of the day. But this is that which was spoken by the prophet Joel; And it shall come to pass in the last days, saith God, I will pour out of my Spirit upon all flesh: and your sons and your daughters shall prophesy, and your young men shall see visions, and your old men shall dream dreams.*
>
> Acts 2:15-17

Merriam-Webster's Dictionary defines *drunk* as "being in a temporary state in which ones physical and mental faculties are impaired by an excess of alcoholic drink." It also means "to be overcome or dominated by a strong feeling or emotion: drunk with power i.e. drunk with joy." This is what we experience in God.

When you are intoxicated in the Holy Spirit, you experience the same effect, but it is without the need for any alcoholic beverage or any other synthetic agent. You are intoxicated with the Holy Spirit.[7]

So, physically speaking, why does a person fall under the power of God? Their physical and spiritual senses are overcome by the glory of God's holy presence.

---

7 Maria Beulah Woodworth, *The Life, Work,and Experiences of Maria Beulah* (St. Louis, Missouri: by the author, 1894), <http://www.merriam-webster.com/dictionary/drunk>.

What Does God's Voice Sound Like?

What does God's voice sound like? This may seem to be off subject, but the truth is that often, when we are slain in the Spirit, we hear God speak to us. In fact, this is one of the greatest benefits of being slain in the Spirit — hearing God speak to you personally.

God desires to speak to you every day. The fact that His voice is heard clearer at the time you are slain in the Spirit is attributable to the fact that as you rest on the floor under the control of the Holy Spirit, you are able to block out any and all distractions.

Moses Heard from God

This happened to Moses:

> *And it came to pass, as Moses entered into the tabernacle, the cloudy pillar descended, and stood at the door of the tabernacle, and the LORD talked with Moses. And all the people saw the cloudy pillar stand at the tabernacle door: and all the people rose up and worshipped, every man in his tent door.* Exodus 33:9-10

Clearly this cloudy pillar was a symbol of the presence of God, and the close proximity of Moses to the presence of God set the stage for God to speak to him. God talked to Moses just as He will talk to you.

You must remember that the reason we fall in the Spirit today is because the presence of the Lord is in close proximity. That's why we can expect the same effect as Moses.

Elijah Heard from God

Another instance when the presence of God engaged a man in this way was recorded in 1 Kings 19:

> *And, behold, the* Lord *passed by, and a great and strong wind rent the mountains, and brake in pieces the rocks before the* Lord*; but the* Lord *was not in the wind: and after the wind an earthquake; but the* Lord *was not in the earthquake: and after the earthquake a fire; but the* Lord *was not in the fire: and after the fire a still small voice. And it was so, when Elijah heard it, that he wrapped his face in his mantle, and went out, and stood in the entering in of the cave. And, behold, there came a voice unto*

him, and said, What doest thou here, Elijah? 1 Kings 19:11-13

God spoke to Elijah in an unexpected tone. The most logical expectation would have been for the God of the universe to speak powerfully. After all, when He spoke to the children of Israel at Mount Sinai, He caused the mountain to smoke and tremble. Now we see the emphasis not on His voice, but on the condition surrounding His speaking. The Lord spoke here in a still, small voice after the earthquake and the fire.

Still, when Elijah heard this voice, he wrapped his face in his mantle. This signified that he felt as if he was covered with the mantle of the Spirit.

So, again, after you fall under the power of the Holy Spirit, don't get up right away. Give the Lord ample time to minister to you. Listen for His whisper, as you lie there on the floor.

After that experience, Elijah went out and stood in the entrance of the cave. This is a type of hearing instructions from God and then coming out of the presence to follow through with the instructions.

Ezekiel Heard from God

It is possible to hear God's voice as majestic and mighty. Ezekiel described the voice of God as magnificent and powerful.

> *And, behold, the glory of the God of Israel came from the way of the east: and his voice was like a noise of many waters: and the earth shined with his glory.* Ezekiel 43:2

To Ezekiel, God's voice seemed like a "*noise.*" *Strong's Hebrew and Greek Dictionary* gives us a clearer understanding of the word *voice* as used here. The transliteration of *noise* is *qol,* and *qol* is from an unused root meaning "to call aloud, proclaim, and thundering":

> *The voice of the* Lord *is upon the waters: the God of glory thundereth: the* Lord *is upon many waters. The voice*

of the L*ORD* *is powerful; the voice of the* L*ORD* *is full of majesty.*

Psalm 29:3-4

The voice of the Lord is "powerful." According to *Strong's Greek & Hebrew Dictionary* this word *powerful* is from *kowach,* from an unused root meaning "to be firm, vigor, or forceful." At times you can expect God's voice to resonate very loudly. He speaks forcefully, with official authority, to bring an understanding in your spirit. That is why some individuals comment that they know something and have nothing in the natural to substantiate what they know. It is just in their "knower" because they have heard from God.

A Voice Like Some We Know?

God's voice may be heard as the familiar voice of some person we know. Some scriptural examples show that sometimes God's voice came across as a man speaking. This was true in the time of Jesus:

And, behold, there appeared unto them Moses and Elias talking with him.
Then answered Peter, and said unto Jesus, Lord, it is good for us to be here: if thou wilt, let us make here three tabernacles; one for thee, and one for Moses, and one for Elias.
While he yet spake, behold, a bright cloud overshadowed them: and behold a voice out of the cloud, which said, This is my beloved Son, in whom I am well pleased; hear ye him. And when the disciples heard it, they fell on their face, and were sore afraid.

Matthew 17:3-6

Another example is found in 2 Peter:

For we have not followed cunningly devised fables, when we made known unto you the power and coming of our Lord Jesus Christ, but were eyewitnesses of his majesty. For he received from God the Father honour and glory, when there came such a voice to him from the excellent glory, This is my beloved Son, in whom I am well pleased. And this voice which came from heaven we heard, when we were with him in the holy mount.

2 Peter 1:16-18

Everyone Has a Different Experience

Everyone experiences God's voice in a different way. At times, it seems that the person God is addressing hears Him exclusively, while others nearby only hear some sort of sound. It also happened this way in Bible days:

"Father, give glory to your name."
A voice from heaven said, "I have given it glory, and I will give it glory again."
The crowd standing there heard the voice and said that it had thundered. Others in the crowd said that an angel had talked to him.
Jesus replied, "That voice wasn't for my benefit but for yours.

John 12:28-30, GWT

As Saul was coming near the city of Damascus, a light from heaven suddenly flashed around him. He fell to the ground and heard a voice say to him, "Saul! Saul! Why are you persecuting me?" ...
Meanwhile, the men traveling with him were speechless. They heard the voice but didn't see anyone.

Acts 9:3-4 and 7, GWT

How God's Voice Communicates with Us

We don't always hear God's voice in a physical sense. Rather He communicates to our spirit, and we suddenly just "know" something:

I will give you a new heart and put a new spirit in you. I will remove your stubborn hearts and give you obedient hearts. I will put my Spirit in you. I will enable you to live by my laws, and you will obey my rules.

Ezekiel 36:26-27, GWT

What His Words Accomplish

When God speaks, it may be both audible and visible, as His words carry both vision and sound. Either way, one word from the Lord can carry you the rest of your life. God's words wash over you and cleanse you from everything that is not consistent with your destiny.

When God speaks, His words have the authority to shape, correct, and create His intended results. His words shall accomplish what He sends them to do. His words are like a capsule that has the capacity to activate His will for your life. It could be compared to a time-release medicine. The words release enough potential daily to establish His will for your life that day.

So, what does God's voice sound like? Each of us may experience Him in a different way.

What Should You Expect While You Are Slain in the Spirit?

What should you expect the Holy Spirit to do while you are under the power? Tragically, most people jump up immediately, and that is a terrible mistake. If God wanted you on the floor, why resist His intentions? It is much better to just lie there for a while to see what He will do. It is better to give the Holy Spirit leeway to minister to you as He wishes. He needs time to do the intended work in you.

We have established the internal effect of the Holy Spirit dwelling in us. When you grasp the meaning of what God has assigned the Holy Spirit to do while you are under His external influence, you will get better results.

You can expect the Lord to work with you, communicating with you as you identify more and more with the Gospel. You can expect Him to produce signs and wonders in your life, as He did with the early believers:

> *So then after the Lord had spoken unto them, he was received up into heaven, and sat on the right hand of God. And they went forth, and preached everywhere, the Lord working with them, and confirming the word with signs following. Amen.* Mark 16:19-20

As we established in Chapter 2, the Holy Spirit will also cause you to conceive. At the same time, He will teach you, remind you, and reveal the mind of the Father to you. He will enable you, cultivate your mind and spirit, and place understanding inside of you. In the process of all this, He will stimulate the fruit of the Spirit in your life.

The Conception

As noted earlier, you conceive when the Holy Spirit comes upon you, and you are impregnated with purpose:

> *And the angel answered and said unto her, The Holy Ghost shall come upon thee, and the power of the Highest shall overshadow thee: therefore also that holy thing which shall be born of thee shall be called the Son of God.*
>
> Luke 1:35

When the power of God comes upon you and conditions are right for conception, you will conceive. As in the natural, pregnancy can only occur when the physical womb is conducive to accept life.

All truth is parallel: The spiritual womb must be suitable to accept the spiritual seed. If you are fertile and all conditions are met in the spirit, you will conceive. Some receive visions and new insight to move into the next level of their process. Others conceive insight to reignite a vision that has been extinguished by time, disappointment, unmet expectations, and gainsayers. Let us look at some of these elements more in detail.

The Holy Spirit Will Give You Words to Speak

The Holy Spirit builds your vocabulary while you are slain in the Spirit, giving you the words to speak at the appropriate time. During this time, the Holy Spirit also cultivates the Word of God you have read, the Word you have heard through the teachings and preachings of others, and the Word you have studied — to grow and strengthen your faith. To the degree that you study the Word of God, to that same degree will be the amount of wisdom in your spiritual reservoir. It is the Word that can change your situation. Reverend Jean Tummings, Pastor of Word Ministries International, Inc. in Brooklyn, New York, always says, "One word from God can change your world."

The Holy Spirit clearly has power to put words in our mouths:

> *But when they shall lead you, and deliver you up, take no thought beforehand what ye shall speak, neither do ye premeditate: but whatsoever shall be given you in that hour, that speak ye: for it is not ye that speak, but the Holy Ghost.* Mark 13:11

It is comforting to know that the Holy Spirit Himself will provide you with a reply that will be adequate for every occasion. You do not have to think beforehand or prepare an answer for anyone.

While you are slain in the Spirit, God may give you power and a special impartation to speak with wisdom, courage, force, and capability at the opportune time.

At times, the Holy Spirit will reveal things in the realm of the Spirit that cannot be uttered in the natural. You will have a consciousness of what He showed you, or what He spoke to you, but you will not be able to relate it to the others.

Some things are better left unspoken. In a case such as this, He will bring you to understand how to put what He has given you in words (at the appointed time). Do not be shaken by this, continue to press forward. It will be revealed to you in God's timing. The words will come to you in God's *kairos* moment.

According to Wikipedia, *kairos* is an ancient Greek word meaning "the right or opportune moment (the supreme moment)." To the ancient Greeks, *kairos* denoted a moment of uncertain time in which something special would happen. What that special something is depends on the current predominate need. Let God's Spirit give you words to speak.

The Holy Spirit Will Teach You

When slain in the Holy Spirit, you are in the school of the Holy Spirit. This is a time that you can be taught, not of man's wisdom, but by the wisdom of the Holy Spirit. Only the Holy Spirit can teach you things that relate to the natural but are conveyed to your spirit:

> *Which things also we speak, not in the words which man's wisdom teacheth, but which the Holy Ghost teacheth; comparing spiritual things with spiritual. But the natural man receiveth not the things of the Spirit of God: for they are foolishness unto him: neither can he know them, because they are spiritually discerned. But he that is spiritual judgeth all things, yet he himself is judged of no man. For who hath known the mind of the Lord, that he may instruct him? But we have the mind of Christ.*
>
> 1 Corinthians 2:13-16

When you are in the presence of the Holy Spirit, He communicates to you spirit to spirit, thereby teaching you things you never could have imagined by natural means.

We are admonished:

> *Search the scriptures; for in them ye think ye have eternal life: and they are they which testify of me.* John 5:39

The Holy Spirit searches your spirit to see what you have invested in it. He then illuminates those scriptures to bring you life. That is why it is important to read scriptures that pertain to your vision. It is also important to commit to memory scriptures that acknowledge the will of God for your life. It is then that you furnish the Holy Spirit with valuable substance to work with:

> *And he that searcheth the hearts knoweth what is the mind of the Spirit, because he maketh intercession for the saints according to the will of God.*
> Romans 8:27

When you are slain in the Spirit, the Holy Spirit searches your heart. He then compares what He knows to be God's will for your life with what He sees in your heart. If there is a discrepancy, He initiates the changes that need to be made in you. This gives you the guidance you need to line up with God's will for your life. The Holy Spirit knows what the Father has in store for you in the future, and He leads you into all truth, even the truth of your destiny.

The Holy Spirit operates like a coach, searching your heart, dealing with doubts, fears, and emotions that prevent you from achieving your goal. He inspires you and wakes up your passions for the things of the Father.

The Holy Spirit Will Remind You

The Holy Spirit will remind you what the Father has spoken to you through His Word. The Holy Ghost teaches by revelation of the Scriptures. He also gives you divine inspiration in regard to your life choices.

Everything you have learned by your senses from childhood about God are memory. God's ways and character are still resident in your spirit. This may not be true on a conscious level, but assuredly it is on an unconscious level.

Once having known Him affects you on a subconscious level. You have God at the foundation of your decision-making capacity. When you are slain in the Spirit, the Holy Spirit can bring to your remembrance what has been deposited in your foundational belief system. As the Scriptures declare:

> *Train up a child in the way he should go: and when he is old, he will not depart from it.* Proverbs 22:6

The Holy Spirit will always remind you of your foundation in God. It is important for parents and guardians to keep children in Sunday School and church at an early stage of development.

For a Christian parent or guardian, the rule of the home should be *"as for me and my house, we will serve the Lord."* The rule of the home should be that attending church is mandatory, never an option. Joshua said it this way:

> *And if it seems evil unto you to serve the LORD, choose you this day whom ye will serve; whether the gods which your fathers served that were on the other side of the flood, or the gods of the Amorites, in whose land ye dwell: but as for me and my house, we will serve the LORD.* Joshua 24:15

If your child lives under a roof you provide, regardless of age — preteen, teen, young adult, or even adult — your standard rule should be: both a worship service and a Bible study at least once a week. When you consider the world we live in today — the culture and the Christ-less attitude of the people around us — being in fellowship with other believers consistently is not an unreasonable requirement.

When our children were home with us, they were required to abide by the worship rule. We provided an opportunity for them to serve God. They did have a choice to attend additional church activities, but the main service and a Bible study were requirements.

If you do not insist on your children attending church, they will stray and fail to get the foundation needed to sustain them later in life. If they are, at some point, drawn away from God and good fellowship and yet hey have the proper Christian foundation, that foundation will bring them back in due course.

The truth is that children who grow up in a Christian household learn Christian principles. They learn to function under godly supervision. They learn problem-solving through Christian principles. During times of trouble, the Holy Spirit will intervene on their behalf. He will remind them of how God came through for them when they were in the Lord. They are no stranger to the ways of God. In due time, the pressures of life will bring them back to something they have seen, heard, or experienced in the past.

While you are slain in the Spirit the Holy Spirit can remind you of any prophecy previously spoken over your life. By reminding you, He reinforces that prophetic word by overlaying the prophetic will of God on your daily life. As the prophetic word is overlaid, a spiritual highway is constructed before you. This highway enables you to spiritually run toward your destiny.

Jesus said:

> *But the Comforter, which is the Holy Ghost, whom the Father will send in my name, he shall teach you all things, and bring all things to your remembrance, whatsoever I have said unto you.* John 14:26

Not only are you reminded of a prophecy that was spoken over your life; you are also endowed with power and given the ammunition to fight against everything that comes into your life that is not consistent with what you know to be the plan of God for you.

God reminds you of what He has spoken to you that otherwise may have been forgotten. You can then do warfare, using the prophecy given to you by a prophet or prophetess of God. If God said it, He will do it. So war with those prophetic words.

Paul wrote to Timothy:

> *This charge I commit unto thee, son Timothy, according to the prophecies which went before on thee, that thou by them mightest war a good warfare.*
>
> 1 Timothy 1:18

During your time of solitude in the presence of God, He touches your memory, to remind you of the victories and triumphs you have seen in the past. He brings to your recall the plan and focus of God and, at such a time, you are receiving comfort and edification.

It is human nature to forget, but the Holy Spirit brings to your remembrance what Jesus spoke to you. He said to His disciples:

I have a lot more to tell you, but that would be too much for you now. When the Spirit of Truth comes, he will guide you into the full truth. He won't speak on his own. He will speak what he hears and will tell you about things to come. He will give me glory, because he will tell you what I say. Everything the Father says is also what I say. That is why I said, 'He will take what I say and tell it to you.

John 16:12-15 GW

While under the power of God, you could be reminded of your destiny, and you may be realigned by the power of God to walk more fully into that destiny.

The Holy Spirit Will Reveal Your Breakthrough

When you are slain in the Spirit, it gives the Holy Spirit the stage backdrop to reveal your breakthrough:

And, behold, there was a man in Jerusalem, whose name was Simeon;

and the same man was just and devout, waiting for the consolation of Israel: and the Holy Ghost was upon him. And it was revealed unto him by the Holy Ghost, that he should not see death, before he had seen the Lord's Christ. Luke 2:25-26

Simeon had long awaited a breakthrough. He knew there was a Savior coming to redeem all mankind. Then, on this particular day, the Holy Spirit came upon him, giving him supernatural knowledge. It was revealed to him that it was the infant he was holding at that moment who would bring salvation to the entire world:

And he came by the Spirit into the temple: and when the parents brought in the child Jesus, to do for him after the custom of the law. Then took he him up in his arms, and blessed God, and said, Lord, now lettest thou thy servant depart in peace, according to thy word: for mine eyes have seen thy salvation. Luke 2:27-30

Revelation of your breakthrough and the supernatural knowledge to realize your wholeness in a certain area can happen when you are slain in the Spirit. Just as with Simeon, the Holy Spirit will reveal the completion of Gods plan for your life. He knows the ending from the beginning.

The Holy Spirit Will Enable You

The Holy Spirit empowers you and creates a new authority in your mind and spirit. He gives you the confidence you need to rise up with the anointing needed to walk with assurance. He makes you more assertive and gives you a greater sense of self-esteem. Once He has your full attention, He enables you to believe the promises of God. He said:

> *But ye shall receive power, after that the Holy Ghost is come upon you: and ye shall be witnesses unto me both in Jerusalem, and in all Judaea, and in Samaria, and unto the uttermost part of the earth.* Acts 1:8

The Holy Spirit Will Reveal His Love

While you are slain in the Spirit, the Father sheds His love in your heart. It is easier in this position to receive love because you are not in a state of resistance. The result is that you will now be able to love those you found hard to accept and show love to before. You will love because issues are dissolved by the Holy Spirit. He saturates your will with the love of God. You could consider this a love overlay in the Spirit. As the Scripture declare:

> *And hope maketh not ashamed; because the love of God is shed abroad in our hearts by the Holy Ghost which is given unto us.* Romans 5:5

The Holy Spirit Will Fill You with Fruit of the Spirit

The Holy Spirit can compensate for any deficit in your character, and you being slain in the Spirit gives Him the freedom and opportunity to shape your fruit.

Let us remind ourselves of the wonderful fruit of the Spirit:

But the fruit of the Spirit is love, joy, peace, longsuffering, gentleness, goodness, faith, meekness, temperance: against such there is no law.

Galatians 5:22-23

When you are slain, the Holy Spirit works on your inner man, instilling the grace you need on a daily bases to help you relate to others. He infuses you with long-suffering, gentleness, goodness, faith, and meekness.

He also provides the fruit you need to walk in victory, helping you gain discipline over yourself. Without temperance or self-control, you would have no victory. He gives you the power to abstain from injurious activity that would endanger your witness. He also gives you control over your temper, your tongue, and your desires:

Now the God of hope fill you with all joy and peace in believing, that ye may abound in hope, through the power of the Holy Ghost. Romans 15:13

The Holy Spirit Will Strengthen You

On this journey, you may get weary. There are strength killers that cross your path daily. These are challenges you must face that are sent to you just to expend your spiritual energy. The psalmist declared:

> *My flesh and my heart faileth: but God is the strength of my heart, and my portion forever.* Psalm 73:26

Your flesh and heart may also fail. According to the *Strong's Greek & Hebrew Dictionary,* this word *faileth* is *kala* which is a primitive root that suggest "to end, to cease, and to be finished, or perish." After a long period of waiting on God, the flesh, being weak and battle-worn, may cease to have the vigor it once had. The heart may feel like it is finished supporting your faith. This is serious because the Scriptures decare that out of your heart flow the issues of life:

Keep thy heart with all diligence; for out of it are the issues of life.

Proverbs 4:23

When you fall under the power, the Holy Spirit strengthens your heart.

The Holy Spirit Will Confirm the Word

The Holy Spirit teaches you the meaning of those things which the Savior has spoken to you, His Word. He will also show you how they apply to your individual life:

Thus saith the LORD the maker thereof, the LORD that formed it, to establish it; the LORD is his name; Call unto me, and I will answer thee, and shew thee great and mighty things, which thou knowest not. Jeremiah 33:3

The book of Jeremiah goes into more detail of what God may be whispering to you while you are slain in the Spirit. Jeremiah the prophet gives us an indication of the

Holy Spirit revealing the promises God has spoken to you.

During the time you are slain in the Spirit, the Holy Spirit can reassure you of what God has spoken to you and you consider *"mighty things."* The *Jamieson-Fausset-Brown Bible Commentary* states that *mighty things* in the Hebrew means "inaccessible things," that is, incredible, hard, to man's way of understanding.[8]

God can speak a promise of recovery as in Jeremiah 33:

> *For thus saith the LORD, the God of Israel, concerning the houses of this city, and concerning the houses of the kings of Judah, which are thrown down by the mounts, and by the sword; They come to fight with the Chaldeans, but it is to fill them with the dead bodies of men, whom I have slain in mine anger and in my fury, and for all whose wickedness I have hid my face from this city.*
>
> Jeremiah 33:4-5

---

8 Jamieson-Fausset-Brown Bible Commentary, < http://www.biblestudytools.com/commentaries/jamieson-fausset-brown/jeremiah/jeremiah-33.html>.

God can speak of healing following punishment:

> *Behold, I will bring it health and cure, and I will cure them, and will reveal unto them the abundance of peace and truth. And I will cause the captivity of Judah and the captivity of Israel to return, and will build them, as at the first. And I will cleanse them from all their iniquity, whereby they have sinned against me; and I will pardon all their iniquities, whereby they have sinned, and whereby they have transgressed against me.*
>
> Jeremiah 33:6-8

God can speak promises of peace and prosperity:

> *And it shall be to me a name of joy, a praise and an honour before all the nations of the earth, which shall hear all the good that I do unto them: and they shall fear and tremble for all the goodness and for all the prosperity*

that I procure unto it. Thus saith the LORD; Again there shall be heard in this place, which ye say shall be desolate without man and without beast, even in the cities of Judah, and in the streets of Jerusalem, that are desolate, without man, and without inhabitant, and without beast, The voice of joy, and the voice of gladness, the voice of the bridegroom, and the voice of the bride, the voice of them that shall say, Praise the LORD of hosts: for the LORD is good; for his mercy endureth for ever: and of them that shall bring the sacrifice of praise into the house of the LORD. For I will cause to return the captivity of the land, as at the first, saith the LORD. Jeremiah 33:9-11

Because God is always concerned with your heartfelt need, He can speak to you the promise of restoration, as in this passage of Jeremiah:

Behold, the days come, saith the LORD, that I will perform that good thing

> *which I have promised unto the house of Israel and to the house of Judah. In those days, and at that time, will I cause the Branch of righteousness to grow up unto David; and he shall execute judgment and righteousness in the land. In those days shall Judah be saved, and Jerusalem shall dwell safely: and this is the name wherewith she shall be called, The* L*ORD* *our righteousness.* Jeremiah 33:14-16

While you are slain in the Spirit, the Holy Spirit ministers to you things you could never figure out on your own. He speaks to you, telling you great and unsearchable things you have not known before. These and other ways the Spirit empowers us are reminders of the importance of allowing Him to always have His way in our lives.

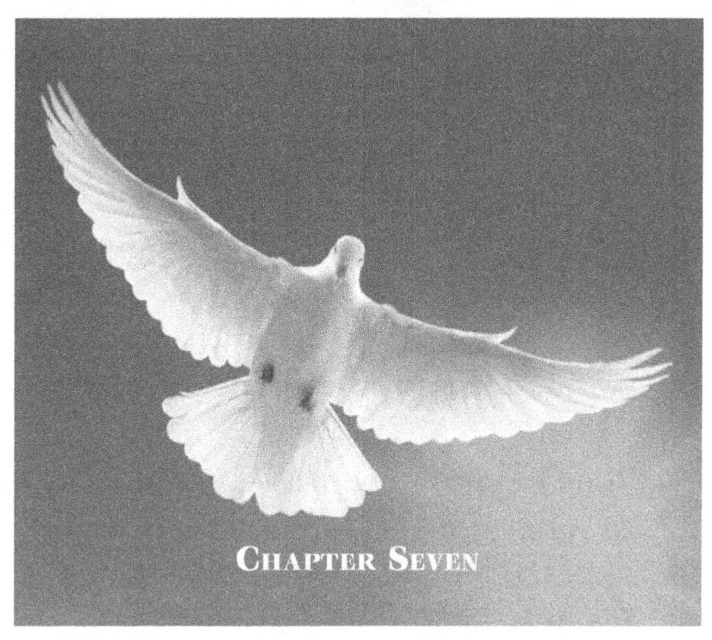

What Is a Trance?

What are trances? Trances are a state of consciousness characterized by extreme disconnection, often to the point of appearing unconscious. A trance is a state resembling deep sleep. It is an out-of-body experience in which one feels they have passed out of the body into another state of being, rapture, and ecstasy. In a general way, trances may be divided into varying degrees of unconscious state.

Trance has been defined as "a half-conscious state seemingly between sleeping and waking in which the ability to function voluntarily may be suspended: a dazed or bewildered condition: a state of complete mental absorption or deep reflection."

When in a trance, you are experiencing a detachment from your physical surroundings, similar to meditation, deep thought, or daydreaming. *Easton's Illustrated Dictionary* defines *trance* as the Greek word *ekstasis,* which denotes the state of one who is "out of himself."[9] *Strong's Greek & Hebrew Dictionary* indicates that *trance* is from *existemi.* It describes a trance as being "a displacement of the mind, i.e. bewilderment, ecstasy.[10]

Such were the trances of Peter and if Paul as recorded in the Acts of the Apostles:

9 *Easton's Illustrated Dictionary,* < http://www.biblestudytools.com/search/?q=trance&s=References&rc=DIC&rc2=EBD>.

10 *Strong's Greek & Hebrew Dictionary,* James Strong (WORDseach Corp: 1980),

On the morrow, as they went on their journey, and drew nigh unto the city, Peter went up upon the housetop to pray about the sixth hour: and he became very hungry, and would have eaten: but while they made ready, he fell into a trance. Acts 10:9-10

And it came to pass, that, when I was come again to Jerusalem, even while I prayed in the temple, I was in a trance; and saw him saying unto me, Make haste, and get thee quickly out of Jerusalem: for they will not receive thy testimony concerning me.
Acts 22:17-18

In this latter passage, we see that God may use a trance to suspend your consciousness so that He can communicate His instructions to you, as He did with Paul in Jerusalem.

Trances Today?

In our era, many people have had visions and fallen into trances. If you are in a trance, it is possible for your eyes to be open and yet you are oblivious to the natural realm. To the physical eye, you would appear to be in a zone of unconsciousness, but you are acutely aware of the Spirit realm. This is described in Numbers:

> *He hath said, which heard the words of God, which saw the vision of the Almighty, falling into a trance, but having his eyes open.* Numbers 24:4

Hearing God's Voice in a Trance

This scripture show us that God's voice can be heard in a trance. Not only can you hear, but you will have knowledge and understanding at that moment as He begins to speak into your spirit:

> *He hath said, which heard the words of God, and knew the knowledge of the most High, which saw the vision of the Almighty, falling into a trance, but having his eyes open.*
>
> Numbers 24:16

Visions and Traces

God may combines vision and trance from time to time. He downloads information to you that would not ordinarily be accepted. A great example is found in Acts:

> *And he* [Peter] *became very hungry, and would have eaten: but while they made ready, he fell into a trance.*
>
> Acts 10:10

You may have a certain core belief that has traditionally been passed down, and it is hard to break such a belief system. God uses vision and trances to break down tradition and strongholds that are in place. The sequential order of this process is: God puts you into a trance and then gives you a vision. A vision is similar to seeing a movie or seeing yourself being actively involved in the movie.

In defense of Peter's action toward the Gentiles, he was convinced that God put His seal of approval on his decision to have fellowship with them. He later gave an account of what had transpired to convince him of this decision, and he included what God had spoken to him while he was in a trance.

Paul did exactly the same thing when challenged by his brothers for having gone to Jerusalem.

The Trance Evangelist

In some eras, trances were even more common. A pioneer evangelists in this country by the name of Maria Woodworth-Etter was known to many as "The Trance Evangelist." In one of her meetings conducted in Fairview, Ohio, in 1883, she wrote that the people confessed sin and "prayed for a baptism of the Holy Ghost and of fire."[11] Fifteen people came to the altar screaming for mercy and fell over in a trance. Even at that early date, Sister Maria called it "the Pentecostal power" adding that "these outpourings of

---

11 < http://enrichmentjournal.ag.org/199901/086woodsworth_etter.cfm>.

the Holy Ghost were always followed by hundreds coming to Christ."[12] She herself fell into trances and remained so for many days. Her faithful followers waited for her to revive, and then the meetings continued.

So what is a trance? It is a deep state of prayer in which a person seems to be unconscious for a time. It is treated in this book simply because a trance often commences when a person is slain in the Spirit.

---

12 Ibid.

How Can You Yield To the Holy Spirit?

We all need to learn the secrets of how to yield to the Holy Spirit. One important thing to remember is that you cannot give and receive at the same time. As Spirit-filled people, we have the ability to pray in the Spirit, speaking mysteries in other tongues:

For he that speaketh in an unknown tongue speaketh not unto men, but unto God: for no man understandeth him; howbeit in the spirit he speaketh mysteries. 1 Corinthian 14:2

But in order to receive from the Lord, put your heart into a spirit of receptivity. Think about receiving instead of giving.

Put Your Heart into a Spirit of Receptivity

Do not speak in tongues, nor pray in the understanding when hands are laid on you. Rather, center your thoughts on godly things, as the Scriptures declare:

Finally, brethren, whatsoever things are true, whatsoever things are honest, whatsoever things are just, whatsoever things are pure, whatsoever things are lovely, whatsoever things are of good report; if there be any virtue, and if there be any praise, think on these things. Philippians 4:7-8

When you concentrate on pleasant things, you can then rest in the peace of God:

> *And the peace of God, which passeth all understanding, shall keep your hearts and minds through Christ Jesus.* Philippians 4:7

This is one time that you come into agreement with your mind, body, soul, and spirit. Listen to the prayer, and set yourself in agreement with the minister. The power of agreement is the place of strength. Join your faith with the minister's faith, and relax in the Lord.

Do Not Resist the Holy Spirit

The greatest hindrance to receiving is to resist. The minister is not trying to push you down. Keep your mind on the fact that God wants to bless you, so open up and receive. Allow the minister to become a conduit for the power of God and the anointing being passed on to you. It is the power of God that you are seeking. The minister is only a conduit to transfer that power from God to you,

Keep your mind, heart, and spirit stayed on God. You mind-set should be: "I surrender to Your will, Lord." The heart should dwell on: "I love Your gifts, Your laws, and Your assignments." And your spirit should reach out to embrace the virtue of God:

> *And Jesus, immediately knowing in himself that virtue had gone out of him, turned him about in the press, and said, Who touched my clothes?*
>
> Mark 5:30

Who Should Lay Hands on You?

There are other things to consider. For instance, who should lay hands on you? You should only allow ministers you respect as being connected to God lay hands on you. This is because you must be comfortable enough to open to their ministry.

The portion of the anointing that is released through them to you is virtue. Jesus explained what happens when God uses a minister to release His virtue. The word for *virtue* used in Mark 5:30 is a familiar Greek word, *dynamis,* which, according to *Strong's Greek & Hebrew Dictionary,* denotes "a force, special miraculous power, and strength." Therefore the minister has the force, special miraculous power, and strength being emitted from their spirit. Who can be on the receiving end of virtue and not have some kind of experience?

Release Your Faith

At the point the minister places hands on you, immediately release your faith to receive all that God has for you.

Remember, you cannot give and receive at the same time. Rest in the Lord. Allow the minister to become the conduit for the power of God. Allow the minister to give to you while you remain quiet and receive with your spirit. Relax, and let the peace of God fill you.

Be open to the Lord to be slain in the Spirit. Yield to God, that He may bless you in any way He desires:

Neither yield ye your members as instruments of unrighteousness unto sin: but yield yourselves unto God, as those that are alive from the dead, and your members as instruments of righteousness unto God. Romans 6:13

Yield in the Greek here is *paristano,* which comes from *para* and *histemi,* which are trasliterated "to be at hand or present yourself." We are invited to present ourselves to God. When you present yourself to Him, you are saying to Him, "Have Your way in my life."

Paul Taught on Yielding

Paul taught the early Roman believers:

Know ye not, that to whom ye yield yourselves servants to obey, his servants ye are to whom ye obey; whether of sin unto death, or of obedience unto righteousness? Romans 6:16

We have a choice. We can yield to whichever power we desire. Yield to God and receive blessing, eternal life, and peace; yield to Satan and receive separation from God, sin, and death. Why would anyone not choose God?

Paul went on:

> *I speak after the manner of men because of the infirmity of your flesh: for as ye have yielded your members servants to uncleanness and to iniquity unto iniquity; even so now yield your members servants to righteousness unto holiness.* Romans 6:19

Draw Nigh To God

As stated in James 4:8, when you are slain by the Holy Spirit, you are drawing closer to God, and He is drawing closer to you. In a sense, you are washing your hands of the world, and the result is that the Lord washes your heart. He said:

> *Draw nigh to God, and he will draw nigh to you. Cleanse your hands, ye*

sinners; and purify your hearts, ye double minded. James 4:8

So lie back and relax. There is no hurry. You are in the presence of God Almighty. Let Him have His way. Allow yourself to be *Overshadowed by the Almighty.*

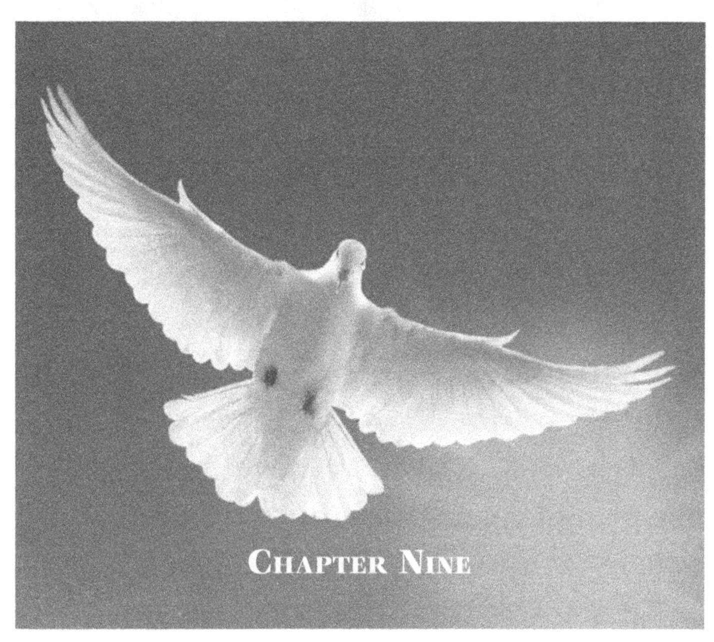

Will You Receive If You Do Not Fall?

Will you receive if you do not fall? Sadly, many have set out to discredit falling under the power of the Holy Spirit, and others focus too much on manifestations such as falling, shaking, and going into trances. These manifestations should not be the main focus, but the fact is that

God will minister to you according to your faith.

According To Your Faith

God is sovereign, and He works whether you fall or not. He can speak, whether you fall under the power or not. But why would you not want to? If this is a blessing from God, and we have found many scriptures from the Bible showing that it is, why would you resist it?

Every experience you have with the Lord will be according to your faith. The expectation you have will permit you to have experiences far beyond your understanding. Pray that you will experience everything that God desires for you.

Personally, I am resolved to experience everything God has for me. I am open to the Spirit at all times. Whenever hands are laid on me, I release my faith. I do not question the mysteries of God. Instead, I am forever looking to see what God wants to do in and through the lives of His people. But be confident in knowing that

God will do what He wants to do, with or without your approval. Your unbelief does not hinder Him.

God will never contradict His Word nor His character, but look to Him for unusual, unprecedented signs and wonders in the days ahead.

Many Have Issues with This Phenomenon

Still many have issues with this and other spiritual phenomena. God said to them through His prophet Isaiah:

> *How horrible it will be for the one who quarrels with his maker. He is pottery among other earthenware pots. Does the clay ask the one who shapes it, "What are you making?" Does your work say to you, "There are no handles"?*
>
> *How horrible it will be for the one who says to his father, "Why did you conceive me?" or to his mother, "Why did you go through labor pains for me?"*
>
> *The* LORD *is the Holy One and the*

> *maker of Israel. This is what the LORD says: "Ask me about what is going to happen to my children! Are you going to give me orders concerning my handiwork?"* Isaiah 45:9-11, GWT

It is fearful thing to resist the Creator. Why risk it? Choose, rather, to be *Overshadowed by the Almighty.*

Other Books by Prophetess Jackie Harewood

Sing Unto the Lord a New Song: An Introduction to Praise and Worship
(0-97-9712623-0-6)

The Violent Take It by Force
(978-1-934769-11-9)

Intercession Builds Bridges: Frequently Asked Questions About Intercession
(978-1-59872-909-2)

I Will Bless THEE

Discovering the Untapped Power of COVENANT

Apostle David Harewood

ISBN 978-1-934769-15-7

Ministry Page

Prophetess Jackie Harewood
3656 Plank Road
Baton Rouge, LA 70805

jharewoodla@cox.net
(225) 772-4552

www.ingramcontent.com/pod-product-compliance
Lightning Source LLC
Chambersburg PA
CBHW031554040426
42452CB00006B/303

* 9 7 8 1 9 3 4 7 6 9 9 9 7 *